STAND UP   SPEAK OUT

WOMEN'S RIGHTS

Virginia Loh-Hagan

the FUTURE is female

FIGHT like a GIRL

#metoo

45 | 45TH PARALLEL PRESS

Published in the United States of America by Cherry Lake Publishing Group
Ann Arbor, Michigan
www.cherrylakepublishing.com

Reading Adviser: Beth Walker Gambro, MS, Ed., Reading Consultant, Yorkville, IL
Book Designer: Jen Wahi

Photo Credits: © Tassii/iStock.com, 4, 14; © Wondermilkycolor/Shutterstock.com, 6; © Angelina Bambina/Shutterstock.com, 8; © Jess Pomponio/Shutterstock.com, 11; © Made360/Shutterstock.com, 12; © NumenaStudios/Shutterstock.com, 17; © CameraCraft/Shutterstock.com, 18; © skynesher/iStock.com, 20; © Everett Collection/Shutterstock.com, 23, 29; © Monkey Business Images/Shutterstock.com, 24; © Zinkevych/iStock.com, 26; © Stephanie Kenner/Shutterstock.com, 30, additional cover images courtesy of iStock.com

45th Parallel Press is an imprint of Cherry Lake Publishing Group.

Library of Congress Cataloging-in-Publication Data

Names: Loh-Hagan, Virginia, author.
Title: Women's rights / Virginia Loh-Hagan.
Description: Ann Arbor, Michigan : Cherry Lake Publishing, 2021. | Series:
   Stand up, speak out | Includes index.
Identifiers: LCCN 2021004965 (print) | LCCN 2021004966 (ebook) | ISBN
   9781534187535 (hardcover) | ISBN 9781534188938 (paperback) | ISBN
   9781534190337 (pdf) | ISBN 9781534191730 (ebook)
Subjects: LCSH: Women's rights–Juvenile literature. | Women–Political
   activity–Juvenile literature.
Classification: LCC HQ1236 .L647 2021 (print) | LCC HQ1236 (ebook) | DDC
   305.42–dc23
LC record available at https://lccn.loc.gov/2021004965
LC ebook record available at https://lccn.loc.gov/2021004966

Printed in the United States of America
Corporate Graphics

About the Author:

Dr. Virginia Loh-Hagan is an author, university professor, and former classroom teacher. She's currently the Director of the Asian Pacific Islander Desi American Resource Center at San Diego State University. She wrote a 45th Parallel Press series about amazing women. She lives in San Diego with her very tall husband and very naughty dogs.

TABLE OF CONTENTS

Activists often work as a group. They have power in numbers.

WHAT IS WOMEN'S RIGHTS ACTIVISM?

Everyone has the power to make our world a better place. A person just has to act. **Activists** fight for change. They fight for their beliefs. They see unfair things. They want to correct wrongs. They want **justice**. Justice is upholding what is right. Activists help others. They serve people and communities.

There are many problems in the world. Activists seek to solve these problems. They learn all they can. They raise awareness. They take action. They inspire others to act.

Activists care very deeply about their **causes**. Causes are principles, aims, or movements. They give rise to activism.

Many activists feel strongly about women's rights. All around the world, women are denied the same rights as men. Women face **sexism**. Sexism is when people are treated unfairly because of their **sex**. Sex refers to being male or female. Men tend to have more **privilege**. Privilege means having power or an advantage.

Women want equal opportunities. They want to control their own bodies. They want to live free from harm.

In this book, we share examples of women's rights issues and actions. We also share tips for how to engage. Your activist journey starts here!

> There is almost the same number of men and women in the world.

GET STARTED

Community service is about helping others. It's about creating a kinder world. Activism goes beyond service. It's about making a fairer and more just world. It involves acting and fighting for change. Choose to be an activist!

O **Focus on your cause!** In addition to the topics covered in this book, there are many others. Other examples include ending violence against women, supporting girls' education, and improving health care.

O **Do your research!** Learn all you can about the cause. Learn about the history. Learn from other activists.

O **Make a plan!** Get organized.

O **Make it happen!** Act! There are many ways to act. Activists write letters. They write petitions. They protest. They march in the streets. They ban or boycott. Boycott means to avoid or not buy something as a protest. They perform art to make people aware. They post to social media. They fight to change laws. They organize sit-in events. They participate in demonstrations and strikes. During strikes, people protest by refusing to do something, such as work.

WE CAN DO IT!

Women around the world had to fight for voting rights.

CHAPTER 1

SUPPORT WOMEN'S SUFFRAGE

Voting lets us choose our leaders. Leaders make laws and policies. In the United States, women's **suffrage** was a long battle. Suffrage is the right to vote. At first, only White men could vote. This wasn't fair. Women's rights activists fought hard. They hosted meetings. They marched. They protested. They changed laws. Women finally received the right to vote in 1920.

Women's suffrage is not just a U.S. issue. Even today, activists around the world are still fighting.

Uganda is in Africa. In 2016, Ugandan women tried to vote. They were beaten. This scared Ugandan women. Women's rights groups complained.

GET INSPIRED

BY PIONEERS IN WOMEN'S RIGHTS ACTIVISM!

O **Susan B. Anthony** fought for women's rights. She traveled to many cities. She gave many speeches. She organized people. She led protests. She started a newspaper. She spread ideas of equality. She led the National American Women's Suffrage Association. She was jailed for voting. She died in 1906. The 19th Amendment passed in 1920. It gave women voting rights. It was known as the "Susan B. Anthony Amendment."

O **Grace Lee Boggs** fought for Asian American rights. She fought for African American rights. She fought for women's rights. She fought for better working and living conditions. She fought for equal pay. She created community groups. She organized people. She spoke at events. She wrote books. She said, "Activism can be the journey rather than the arrival." She died in 2015. She was 100 years old.

WE CAN
TAMIKA MALLORY
AND
THE WOMEN'S VOTE
WE WILL!

● Some governments try to keep specific groups from voting to ensure certain people win elections.

They trained people to watch over the elections.

Afghanistan is in the Middle East. In 2019, Afghanistan required voters to be photographed. Activists think this stops women from voting. Some Afghan women cover their faces outside the home. They can't show their faces to men. More than 15 women's rights groups wrote to officials. They're fighting to get rid of the photo requirement.

Vatican City is in Rome, Italy. It's the center of the Roman Catholic Church. It doesn't hold elections for its citizens.

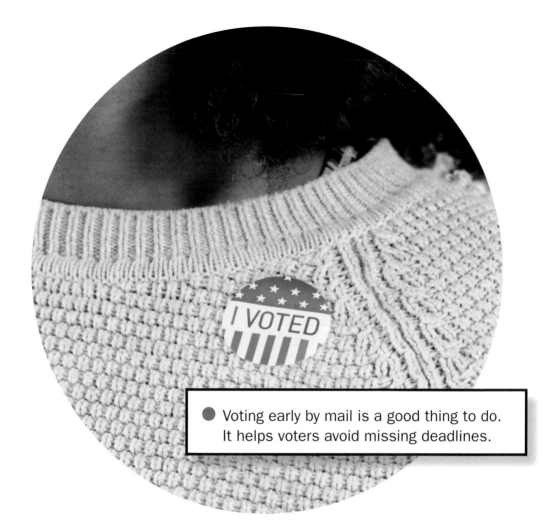

Voting early by mail is a good thing to do. It helps voters avoid missing deadlines.

So it's one of the last places in the world that doesn't allow women to vote. A group of cardinals elect the pope. The pope is the Catholic Church's top leader. Since the Catholic Church does not allow women to be cardinals, only male church leaders can vote. Activists are fighting this rule. They want female church leaders to have voting rights. They believe women's voices should be heard during decisions. They sign petitions. They host rallies.

Stand Up, Speak Out

The United States Postal Service (USPS) is in charge of our mail. Mail service is important for elections. Some people mail their **ballots**. Ballots are voter cards. Mail-in ballots let sick or elderly people vote. They help people who have several jobs. They help people who take care of children. Activists want to protect voting rights. They support the USPS. You can help!

> Buy stamps. Encourage other people to buy stamps. Learn about how to submit stamp designs. Host a stamp-designing party. Work to get more women featured on stamps.

> Call politicians. Ask them to support more USPS drop boxes in your area. Ask them to give the USPS more funding.

Hillary Clinton is famous for saying, "Women's rights are human rights."

CHAPTER 2

GET WOMEN ELECTED

Women having voting rights is important. It's also important to have women leaders. There are more male leaders than women leaders. This is unfair. The limits to women leaders are often called a glass ceiling. The glass ceiling is a **metaphor**. It's a way to describe something by calling it something else. The glass ceiling is the invisible barrier that stops women from getting elected. It stops them from advancing in their careers.

In 2016, Hillary Clinton tried to break "the highest, hardest glass ceiling." She ran for U.S. president. She was the first woman to do so with a major political party. She inspired many women. Many women's marches protested her loss in the election. A record number of women ran for office. The #MeToo movement started. Women refused to be silent

GET INSPIRED

BY LEGAL VICTORIES

○ The Equal Rights Amendment (ERA) gives equal legal rights to women. In 1923, Alice Paul and Crystal Eastman wrote the first version. It didn't pass Congress until 1972. Then, it was sent to the states to approve. Many opposed it. But activists keep fighting. They won't stop until it's part of the U.S. Constitution.

○ Lilly Ledbetter worked at a tire factory. Her boss didn't think women should work there. He didn't pay her fairly. Ledbetter sued. She lost her court case. But in 2009, Congress passed the Lilly Ledbetter Fair Pay Act.

○ Saudi Arabia had banned women from driving. Saudi Arabian women activists started the Women to Drive Movement. In 1990, they drove in public. They were put in jail. In 2007, they petitioned the king. They demanded that women have the right to drive. More women protested. In 2018, the ban on women driving was lifted.

victims of sexual violence. They wanted to heal. They wanted to support other survivors. They stood together. They fought against the **patriarchy**. Patriarchy is a government controlled by men.

In 2020, Kamala Harris became the U.S. vice president. She was the first woman and the first Black and South Asian person to be vice president. She said, "While I may be the first woman in this office, I will not be the last." More women in charge means more support for women.

● Women leaders tend to face more criticism than men.

Women need funding to run for office. They don't have the same access to money as men.

The United Nations (UN) Women program supports women around the world. It provides training on women's rights. This program inspired Coumba Diaw. She became a mayor of a community in Senegal, Africa. Diaw taught women about health. She hosted weekly markets for women to earn money. She set up drinking taps so women wouldn't have to walk for hours to get water.

Stand Up, Speak Out

Governments need to serve the people. They also need to look like the people they serve. Women leaders tend to support women's issues. They also support other women. Activists want to get more women elected to office. You can help!

> Check out women running for office in your area. Learn about their ideas. Make posters for them. Post on social media to support them.

> Get more young people to vote. Young voters aged 18 to 25 tend to vote for women and people of color. Work with an adult to host workshops. The workshops can spread information on how to register to vote.

> Make voting guides. Include women and people of color.

Women can be leaders in all fields. They must be supported.

CHAPTER 3

FIGHT FOR EQUAL PAY

Usually, men get better jobs than women. They get promoted more. They rise in the ranks faster. They have more power. They make more money. Even when men and women do the same work, men still get paid more. This is not right. Activists want equal pay for equal work.

The U.S. women's soccer team wins more games than the men's team. But they're paid less. They're fighting for equal pay. Their battle started in 2016. The top players filed a complaint. They talked on TV shows. They made speeches. They rallied support from others. They inspired other female athletes.

Female movie stars also have to fight for equal pay. Male actors tend to make a lot more money.

21

GET IN THE KNOW

KNOW THE HISTORY

○ **1848** The first women's rights meeting was organized by Elizabeth Cady Stanton and Lucretia Mott. It was called the Seneca Falls Convention. It was held in New York. This event sparked many years of activism.

○ **1893** New Zealand became the first country to grant women voting rights. Kate Sheppard was the leader of the New Zealand suffrage movement.

○ **1956** More than 20,000 women marched in South Africa. They protested against laws requiring Black people to have passes to move within the country. The women stood silently for 30 minutes. Then, they sang in protest. They said, "You strike a woman. You strike a rock." This became their motto.

○ **1963** The Equal Pay Act passed. This law bans sex-based pay discrimination. Activists use this law as a tool. They take employers to court. Employers are bosses.

○ **1968** Shirley Chisholm was the first African-American woman elected to the U.S. Congress. She was also the first African American to run for U.S. president. She fought for equal rights.

Beyoncé is a modern feminist. She empowers women through her songs.

Many female actresses are boycotting. They're refusing to do movies unless they get equal pay. They have **allies**. Allies are supporters. Some male actors are also making a stand. They won't do movies unless their female co-stars get equal pay.

Beyoncé is a singer and movie actress. In 2014, she wrote a report. She wrote, "Unless women and men both say [pay inequity] is unacceptable, things will not change. Equality will be achieved when men and women are granted equal pay and equal respect."

 In the United States, women make about 79 cents for every dollar made by men. Women of color make less than White women.

Stand Up, Speak Out

Some people don't like talking about money. They think money should be private. We should be smart about money. We should be open. Knowing how much people make helps decrease the **wage** gap. A wage is how much people make for work. Activists want to make things fairer for women. You can help!

> Teach **negotiating** skills. Negotiating means working to agree. Some women are shy about asking for more money. Learning to talk about money is an important skill.

> Celebrate International Equal Pay Day on September 18. Host meetings. Ask successful women to share their stories.

> Research a company. Learn what men make. Learn what women earn. Write to the company leaders. Ask them to pay women equally.

In 2013, the United States lifted its ban on women in combat.

CHAPTER 4

PROMOTE WOMEN IN THE MILITARY

Many countries are relaxing their bans on women in the military. More female soldiers serve than ever before. But there's room for more. There also needs to be more female military leaders.

India has a large army. Less than 4 percent are women. Female officers got lawyers. They fought for more rights in the courts. In 2020, India's Supreme Court supported equal rights in the armed forces. Indian women can earn the same ranks as men. They can get the same pay. But India still bans women from **combat**. This means they can't fight on the battlefields. Some people don't think women are strong enough. Activists want to change how people think of women.

U.S. Army Captain Katie Wilder was the first woman

GET INVOLVED

There are several groups fighting for women's rights. Connect with them to get more involved.

○ **Dress for Success** empowers women. Its workers help women earn money. They give women work clothes and provide job training.

○ **Girl Up** provides leadership training. It provides community organizing skills and communication skills. Its motto is, "When girls rise, we all rise."

○ **Girls Who Code** empowers young women to get jobs in STEM. STEM is Science, Technology, Engineering, and Math. Girls Who Code provides coding classes.

○ **The League of Women Voters** used to be the National American Women's Suffrage Association. The League formed in 1920. Its members support women in politics. They help register voters. They provide voting guides. They help get women elected.

○ **NOW** is the National Organization for Women. It's the largest group of women activists. Its members fight against sexism. They fight for equal rights. They fight for better services for women.

to graduate from special forces training. In 1980, Wilder applied to the special forces program. She was denied because she was a woman. She fought back in court. She won. She passed the training. But she was not allowed to graduate. She fought back. Today, women continue to fight for their right to serve their country.

● Women held many roles during World War I. These jobs included nurses, mechanics, and clerical workers.

Women were banned from military schools. Ruth Bader Ginsberg fought for the fair treatment of women. She was the second female U.S. **Supreme Court Justice**. Justices are judges in the country's highest court. In 1996, she wrote the decision that allowed women to be admitted to the Virginia Military Institute.

● Ginsberg was known for saying, "I dissent."

HONOR RBG'S WISHES

Stand Up, Speak Out

Women in the military face many challenges. They're underestimated. Sometimes, they're not respected. Sometimes, they're abused. Activists want to help women achieve their goals. You can help!

> Call or write politicians. Ask for better gender-specific gear for troops. This means having body armor and helmets that fit different bodies.

> Teach yourself and others how to be more **inclusive**. Inclusive means making everyone feel welcome. Use inclusive language. Practice respectful behaviors. Work to stop sexism.

> Write to women in the military. Thank them for their service. Encourage them to keep fighting.

GLOSSARY

activists (AK-tih-vists) people who fight for political or social change

allies (AL-eyes) supporters

ballots (BAL-uhts) voting cards

boycott (BOI-kot) to refuse to buy something or take part in something as a protest to force change

causes (KAWZ-es) the reasons for activism

combat (KOM-bat) fighting on the battlefield

inclusive (in-KLOO-siv) welcoming to all

justice (JUHSS-tiss) the upholding of what is fair and right

metaphor (MET-uh-for) a way of describing something by calling it something else

negotiating (ni-GOH-shee-ate-ing) working to agree, to compromise

patriarchy (PAY-tree-ar-kee) a government controlled by men

privilege (PRIV-uh-lij) a special advantage or unearned power

sex (SEKS) being male or female

sexism (SEK-sih-zuhm) the unfair treatment due to a person's sex

strikes (STRYKES) organized protests where people refuse to work

suffrage (SUHF-rig) the right to vote in elections

Supreme Court Justice (SUH-preem KORT JUHSS-tiss) a judge in the U.S. highest court

wage (WAYJ) the amount someone is paid for doing work

LEARN MORE!

Gillibrand, Kristen, and Maira Kalman (illust.). *Bold & Brave: Ten Heroes Who Won Women the Right to Vote.* New York, NY: Alfred A. Knopf, 2018.

Hopkinson, Deborah. *What Is the Women's Rights Movement?* New York, NY: Penguin Workshop, 2018.

Kendall, Mikki, and A. D'Amico (illust.). *Amazons, Abolitionists, and Activists: A Graphic History of Women's Fight for Their Rights.* Berkeley, CA: Ten Speed Press, 2019.

INDEX